We hope you enjoy coloring this book.

Download some extra

free coloring patterns

and get news of upcoming books at

www.scribblepresscoloring.com/free-download

SWEDEN

SWEDEN

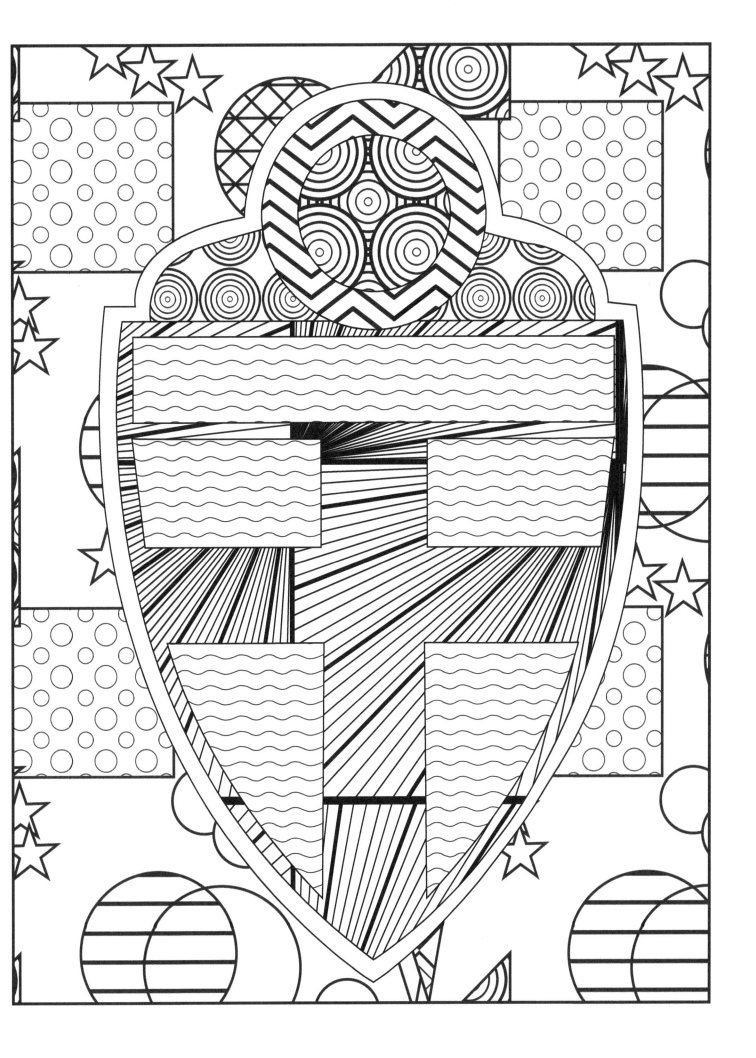

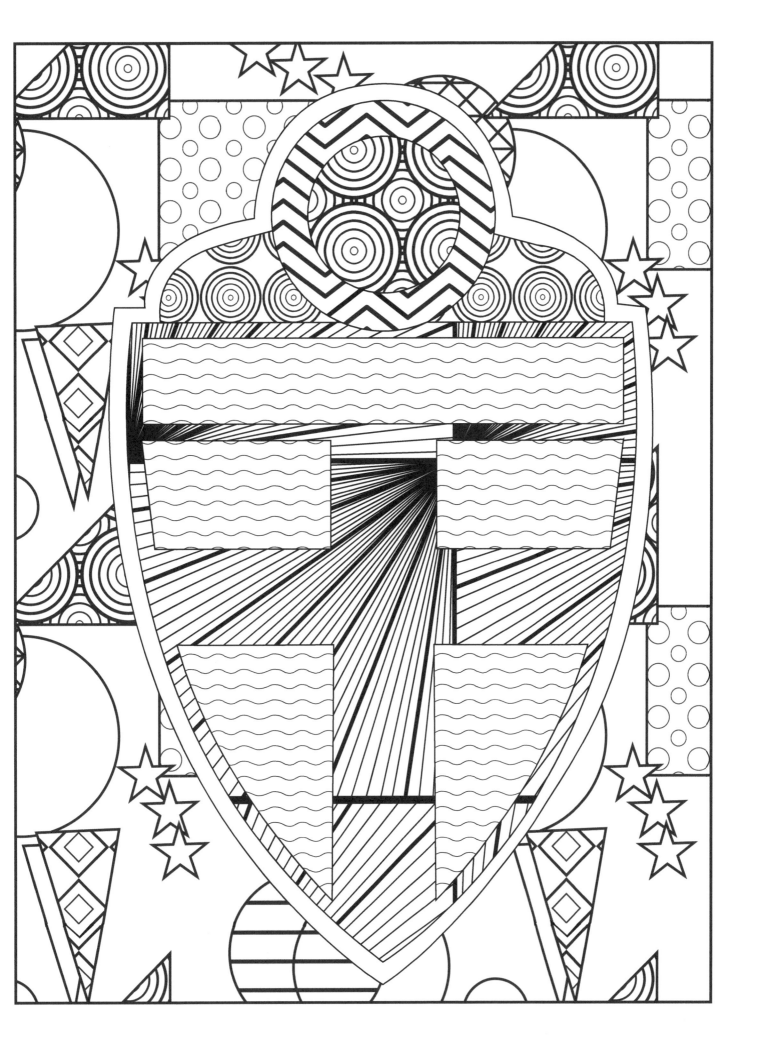

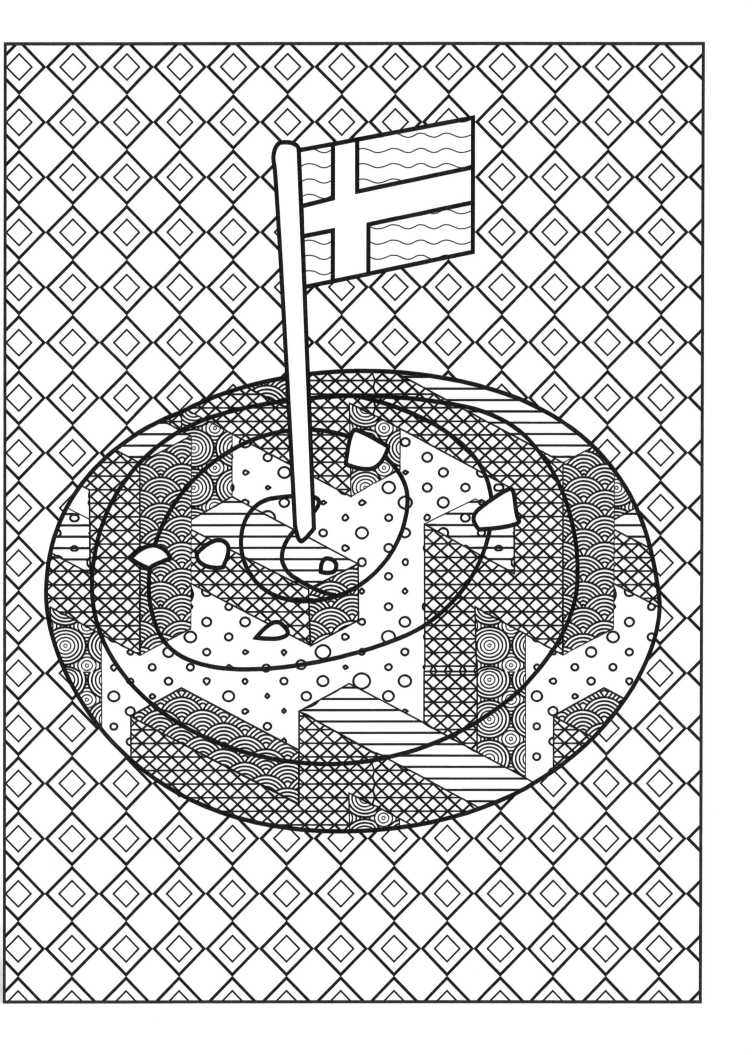

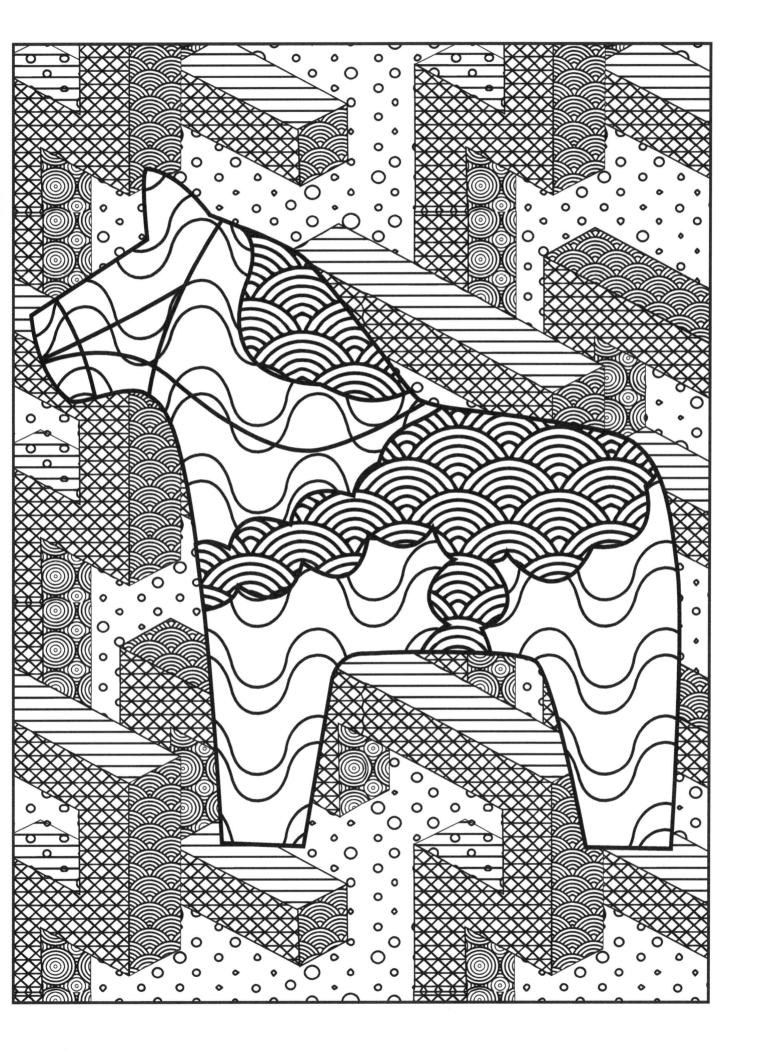

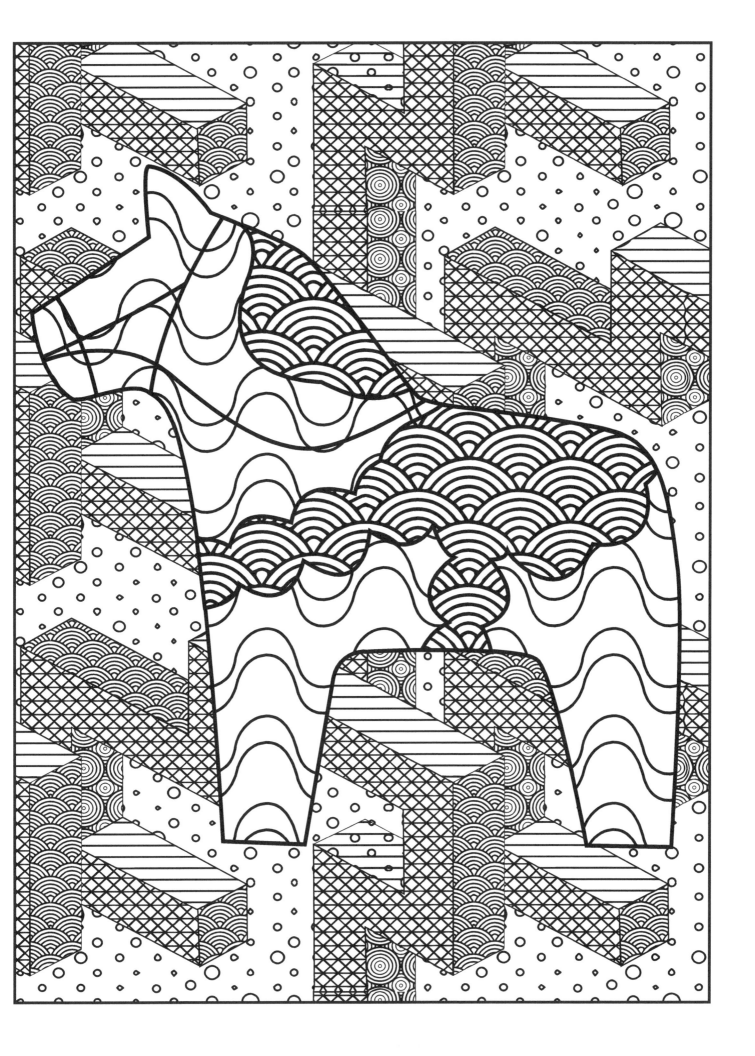

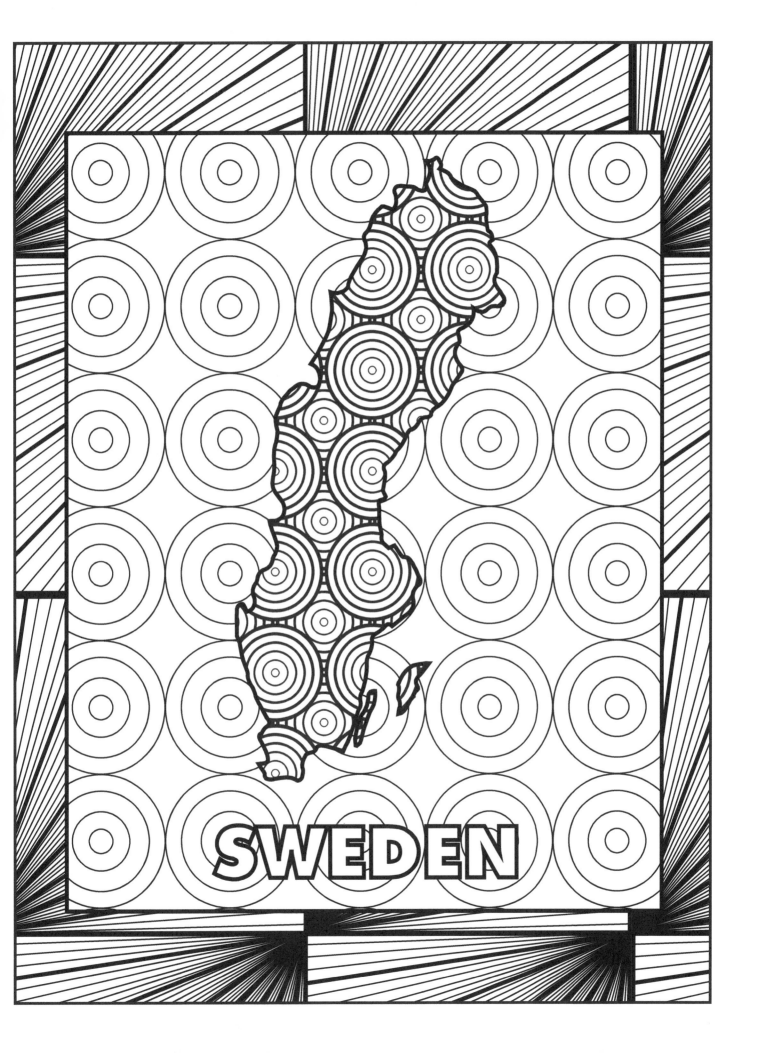

SWEDEN

SWEDEN

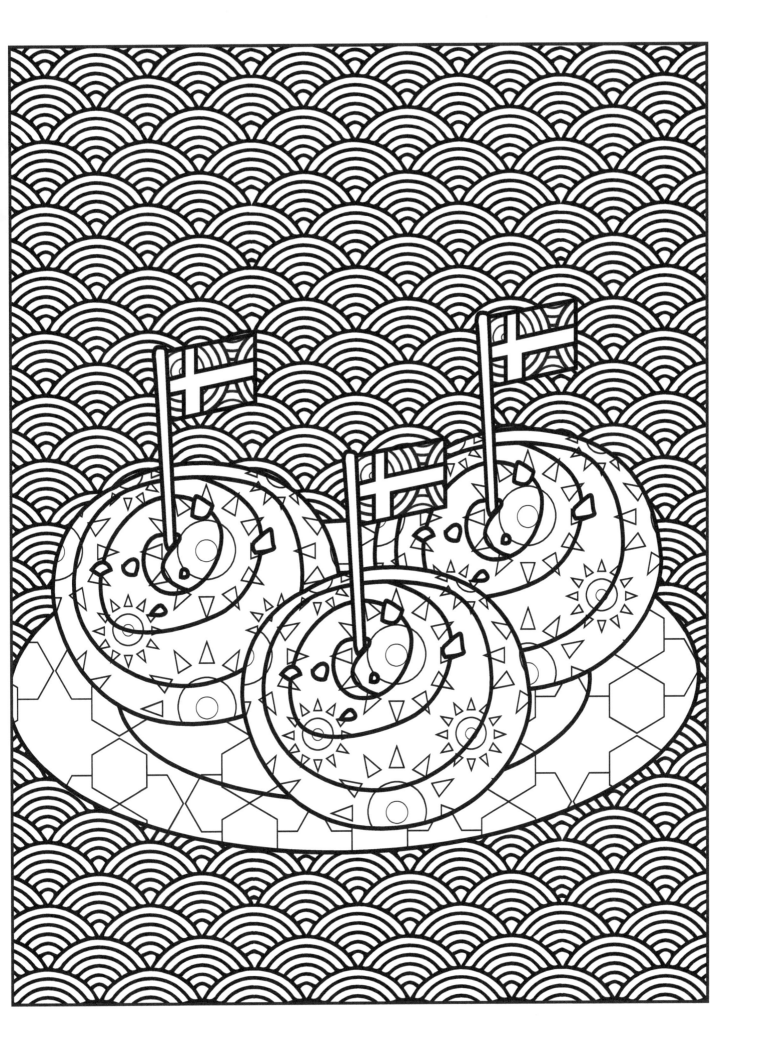

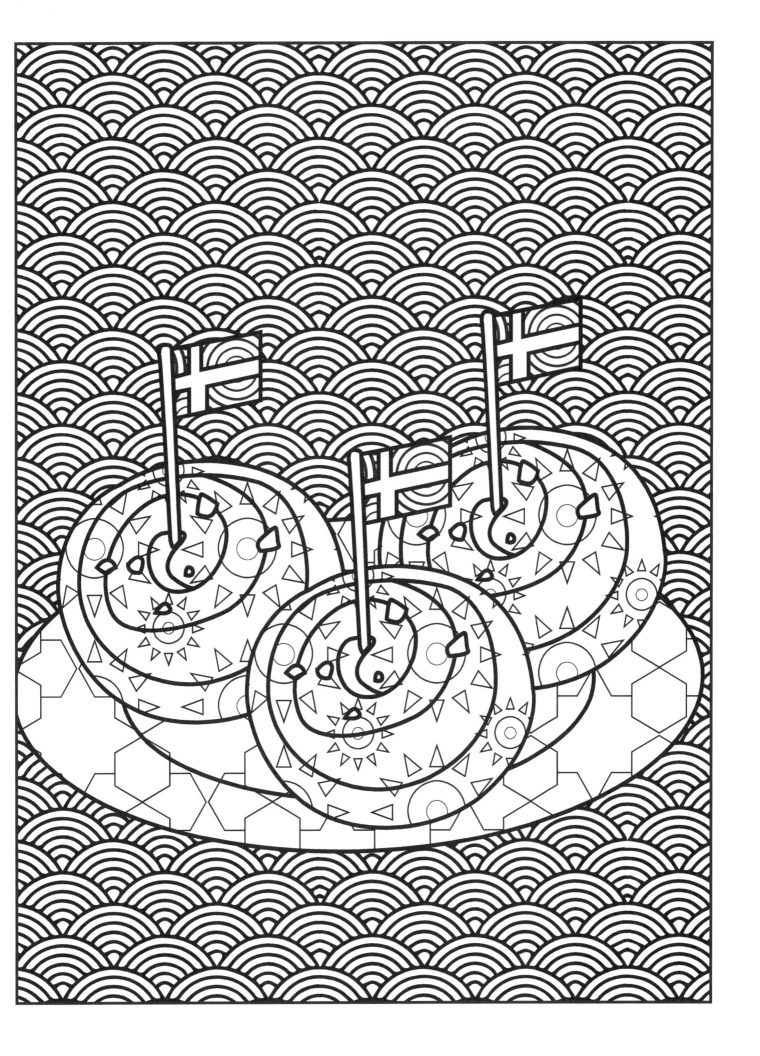

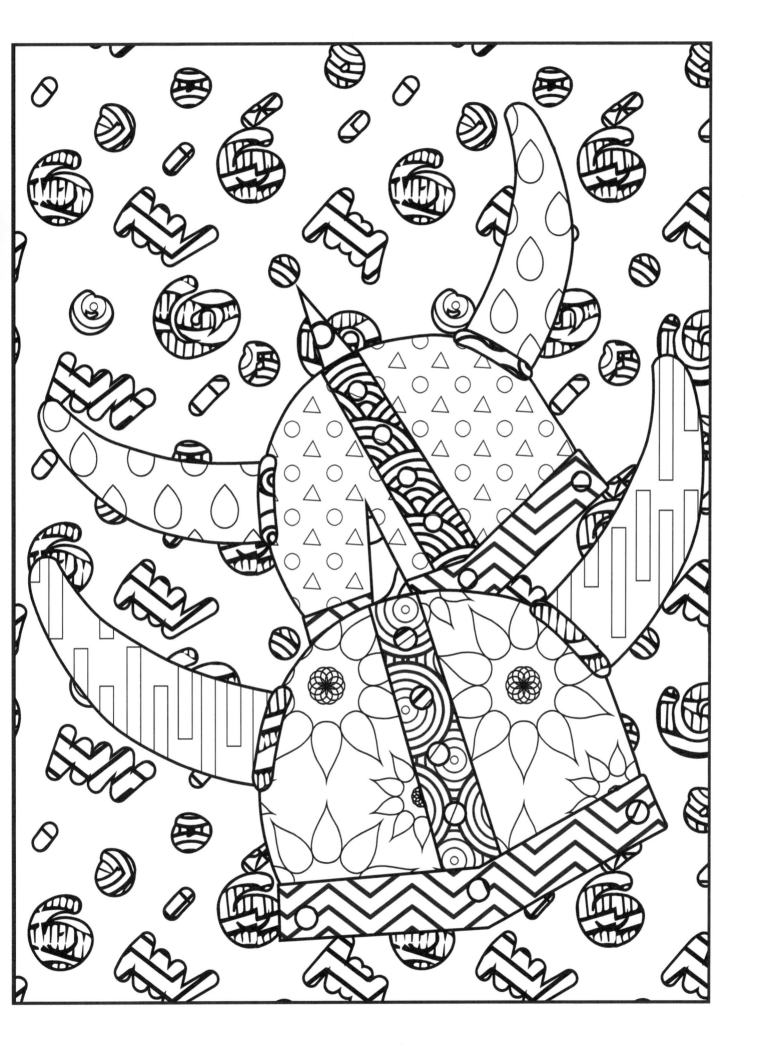

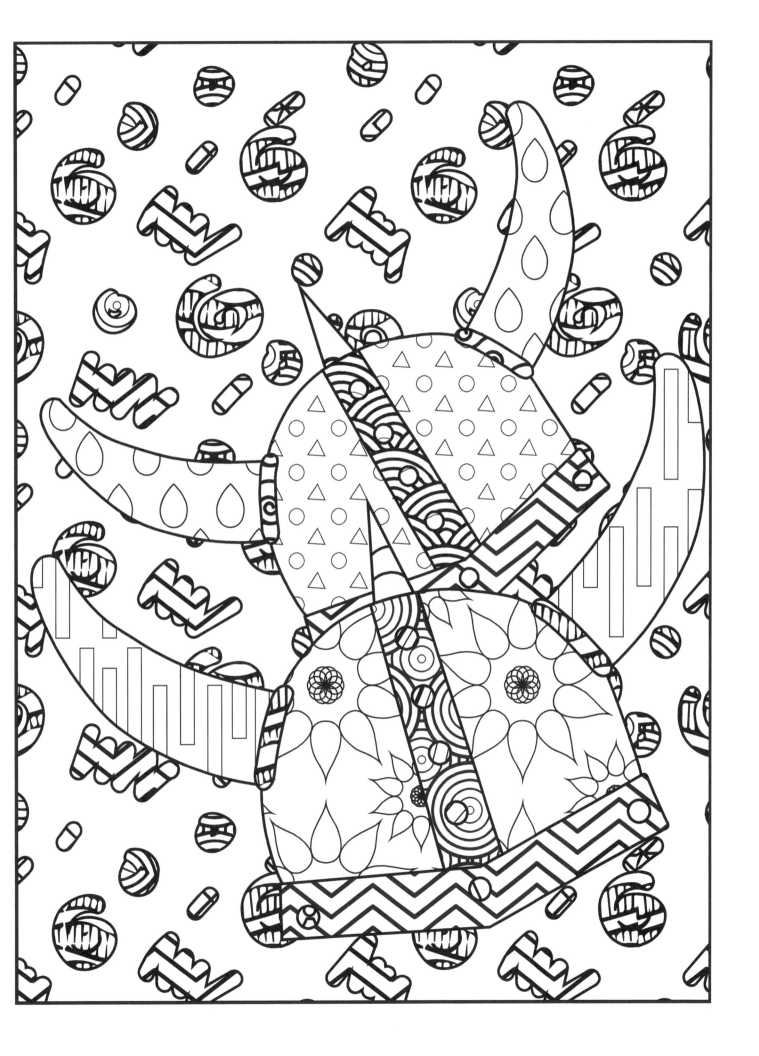

Made in United States
Troutdale, OR
11/25/2023

14947621R00038